Twitch and Shout, Hallelujah, Amen

Twitch and Shout, Hallelujah, Amen

Poems of Love, Forgiveness, and Living with Tourette's Syndrome

GREGORY JOHN NASHIF

Foreword by Scott Waters

RESOURCE *Publications* · Eugene, Oregon

TWITCH AND SHOUT, HALLELUJAH, AMEN
Poems of Love, Forgiveness and Living with Tourette's

Resource Publications
An Imprint of Wipf and Stock Publishers
199 W. 8th Ave., Suite 3
Eugene, OR 97401

www.wipfandstock.com

PAPERBACK ISBN: 978-1-5326-7297-2
HARDCOVER ISBN: 978-1-5326-7298-9
EBOOK ISBN: 978-1-5326-7299-6

Manufactured in the U.S.A.   01/10/19

My Tribute

Sometimes, when life gets the best of us, and we get lonely, down and feeling afraid of what things in life will come my way.

And when it looks like all things are lost, at that moment The Lord brings to me a kind and loving spirit, with a firm but gentle hand;

Who shares with me the willingness of his human heart to guide me through the darkest moments of my life.

To teach me about integrity, and honesty. Leading me to find the Lord's ever abiding love.

Because of your kindness, and gentle heart, you have taught me that I am never alone, if I have a friend in Jesus.

I want you to know how much you mean to me, and how much I will miss your gentle touch, your warm smile, and those special hugs.

And when I die, and Leave this earth, as His little child now safely in the soft embrace of Jesus' arms. I will come ever close and softly whisper in His ear, and let the Lord know how good you truly were to me.

And Jesus smiled.

In Jesus Name this Book is Written

This volume of poetry is dedicated to all the "unlovelies" of the world, who because of their disabilities have been outcasts in society

And to all my friends who over the years have loved, supported me, and have given me comfort, through all the trials of my life.

For in Him we live and move, and have our being, as certain also your own poets have said, "for we are his offspring."

—ACTS 17:28

Table of Contents

Part the Third: Living with Tourette's—
Finding Love, Acceptance, and Forgiveness

Epilogue: Conclusion of the Whole Matter

Foreword

To THE READER OF this sacred story:

What you are about to read is a non-linear story written in some prose but mostly verse. This poetic journal is written out of a lot of experience in the life of a man who from an early age, was misunderstood. Greg consistently was talked down to and mocked for his differences.

Greg Nashif started his life with Tourette's syndrome. At the time of his adolescence he was abused. This compounded the nature of his rejection and pain as he was not only told he was worthless, but he became a victim of people who exploited his vulnerability. He has faced a lot of rejection and pain.

I've gotten to know Greg as a friend for the last 7 years or so, walking alongside him in his angst and frustration. This time I've spent with him has helped me grow in empathy and love. His hurt has been a point of which he has grown and matured into a grace-filled man; learning to forgive and love in the direst of circumstances. This means he has eyes and ears to find the least of these and shine the love of God in their experience.

I cannot capture the level of love in Greg's heart with words. What I can say is that amidst the oppression he faced, he always ended up turning to God to speak life into the despair that consumed him. It may have taken him years for somethings and months for others. His journey and internal process which you are about to read is so vulnerable and filled with courage. I dare you to read it without shedding a tear.

Ultimately this is a story of victory. The verses Greg wrote share his story about God's redeeming grace. I hope you see yourself somewhere in the verses and can conclude that he ultimately kept coming back to.

God is the one who redeems and makes all things new. So, while you read, enjoy your own twitch and shout for the work God has and is doing in your life.

Blessings,
Scott Waters, MA, LPC

Introduction

I THOUGHT LONG AND hard about how to write this poetry book;
Where do I start? I am not sure where to begin. . .
"Begin at the beginning, young fella!" an old man yelled out.
"Who's there?" I questioned.
"Just—Start—From—the Beginning," said the old man.
I think I am finally going crazy. Now I am hearing all kinds of voices, just start from the beginning; of course, you always start from the beginning, What a cliché. That is of course the normal thing to do, is it not?
"Hey voice" I shouted out.
"I am listening," said the old man.
"I can tell you, with absolute certainty, that I am not a cliché, and I am not normal either! Urp, Urp, yelp, yelp yelp . . . " Tic, tic, tic . . . tap, tap, tap. I TWITCH and SHOUT.
"Ok young fella, you made your point, now stop all that nonsense, all that ruckus, you're driving me Insanitatible."
"Urp, Urp, yelp, yelp yelp . . . " Tic, tic, tic. . . tap, tap, tap; TWITCH and SHOUT.
"Fella please stop that now, are you trying to annoy me?"
"Urp, Urp, yelp, yelp yelp . . . " Tic, tic, tic . . . tap, tap, tap; TWITCH and SHOUT.
The voice yelling out for the final time, "STOP THAT INSANITY!!!!"
"But I cannot, "I replied," I simply can't get away from you, because you are me! You see, I am Tourette's."
For years, I just kept talking to myself; feeling sorry for myself. "Why me? Why do I have to be burdened with this horrible thing called Tourette Syndrome?"
Tourette's is not fatal, although I did think at various times, how much easier it would be just to pack up my bags, and hitchhike to a land of peace

and joy; a spirit land with no pain or suffering, no noises or tics, twitching or shouting. It was all Psych-Illogical to me until 1970, when I accepted Christ the Lord into my life and began a journey to salvation, hope, peace, joy, and redemption.

I have been through many struggles, trials and tribulations. In them I always end up remembering that the Lord does not allow me to go through anything I cannot handle: with each trial He offers me a way of escape, so I can bear it. (1 Corinthians 10:13)

As I look at all the events I have been through, I can see what an awesome adventure of Love, Forgiveness and Living with Tourette's it has been. These writings are little glimpses into my life: some of these poems were written during times of distress, some brought comfort to my soul and uplifted my spirit.

It is my hope and prayer that this book inspires you to be the men and women that God desires us to become. That we learn compassion for those who are struggling, without judgment. That we extend mercy and grace, not only to others but also to ourselves. In doing so, we transcend our frail humanity and embrace the wonderful Joy that is Christ.

And so, it begins . . .

Poetry is the expression of a man; it is the extension of his soul
—Gregory J Nashif

Carried on the Wind

"Holy Spirit dwell inside me,
fill me with your pure desire."
I raise my hands in worship praising,
with the tongues of holy fire.

Holy Spirit let your peace prevail
upon this earth so dark with hate;
allow your love and word avail,
with your spirit this holy fate.

All prophets of this world ignite!
Spirit aflame the heart and mind!
Pierce with the sword of truth and might
and slay the souls of all mankind.

The Lord is faithful by all measure,
reaching the world face to face.
For His wisdom is our treasure,
which inspires His Holy Grace.

Which inspires His Holy Grace

Anthem

How Great is God and His creation!
His Works performed among every nation,
He has given us life upon this earth;
And in our hearts His eternal birth.
How Great is God!

His Spirit moved upon the waters deep,
He spoke the word and the light did weep;
By his hands the worlds were framed,
And through his Son the world was tamed.
How Great is God!

Every star, He calls by name,
He knows the number of the same.
He knows our hearts and our minds,
He frees the one whose thoughts are blind.
How Great is God!

How Great is God and His creation!
His Works performed among every nation.
He has given us life upon this earth;
And in our hearts His eternal birth.
How Great is God!

Jesus healed the sick and raised the dead,
Through his Father's will his blood was shed.
Breathing, at the last, with forceful breath;
He died, He arose, He conquered Death.
How Great is God.

As I bow my head in prayer,
I know my God and feel his care.
There is one last sigh for my soul;
I live by faith and now I know,
How Great is God.

Part the First

Living with Tourette Syndrome

Tourette Syndrome

noun.

a neurological disorder characterized by recurrent involuntary movements, including multiple neck jerks and sometimes vocal tics, as grunts, barks, or words, especially obscenities.

Discovered by French neurologist George Gilles de la Tourette in 1885

Also called Tourette's disease.

Dictionary.com Unabridged Based on the Random House Un-abridged Dictionary, © Random House, Inc. 2018

My Life

It has been an interesting life, living with Tourette's at times has been a strange adventure; sometimes like a merry-go-round, like a circle with no beginning and no end. Other times it is a roller coaster ride, or an unfinished jigsaw puzzle with its pieces scattered; and me trying with all my heart to pick them up one by one and make them fit into a clear picture.

I'll live with these ticks all my life.
I cannot escape the hardship and strife
this twitch and shout bring to me every day.
Is there any peace coming my way?

I never get used to people's stares,
The laughing, the mocking; nobody cares.
My body is tired and so torn apart
Tears fall from what is left of my heart.

Is there a hope I can find somewhere?
Is there a breath I can take to ease my despair?
If much weeping comes in the night without warning,
Will joy come my way in the light of the morning?

Marbles

I am just kid, a boy so young and ever so naïve.

On the playground at school, I sit alone and watch as kids are having fun: kick ball, marbles,

little girls playing hopscotch.

As I sit and wait, my head begins to tic and quake, and kids stop and look.

One shouts out "You're a freak!" Another throws a boy's coat and hits me in the head.

"Now you have his germs!" he calls.

After some time, one little boy comes and sits by me,

"I know you are a nice guy and all. I don't understand, what makes you jump around so much.

It seems kind of funny, you know?" he asks.

I replied, "I don't understand either, but it is just who I am, the way I am.

But hey, will you be my friend?"

The little boy explains, "As I said I know you are a nice guy, and I do like you a whole lot, and would very much like to be your friend."

"But," he continues, "I can't right now. I am afraid of what my friends will say, what these kids might do to me, the friend of a freak. Then I will be just as alone as you."

The little boy got up from the bench, simply smiled and walked away, and joined his buddies for a rousing game of marbles.

And then Again . . . .

It was recess
10 years old,
On the playground.
Lonely time,
My tics were strong, Out of control,
Bullies, oppressors Never cease
And the teachers just looked the other way.

I felt alone,
Not a quiet loneliness,
A loudly clanging fear,
That would last
Until the clock rang out, "it is finished."
Relief, taking a breath, a sigh,
"I made it through another day"

The Rain

Sometimes I just sit back and wonder why, I am the way that I am. I love to just be outside and watch as the clouds pass by, and then see the sky get dark, a little thunder, a little lightning, and then the pouring rain. I sat and wondered, "are those the tears that angels shed for me."

I think It is going to rain today,

I better cover my head as I walk the highway,

this road is long and the way uncertain.

I better wear a coat to keep warm from the coldness of purging winds.

I think it is going to rain today,

The sky looks cloudy and gray, the sun is gone, the earth dark;

I better bring a light, for the journey is long,

And darkness seems to follow my path.

I think it is going to rain today,

I better wear my boots, to keep my feet dry.

For these clouds bring pools of muddy water,

The road is rocky, and every step is life.

I think it is going to rain today,

A few tiny drops have already speckled by clothes;

The dry earth suddenly becomes soft; the dust is settled;

There is no turning back; for in every movement there is time.

Possessed

In my distress, the Lord said to me, "Listen my son, to the wisdom I have to share with you. For my voice is sweet, and my sayings are simple. There will come a time when my children will not understand your tics and noises, your twitch and your shout. In their human frailty they will mock you and call you demon possessed. And in their ignorance, shall lay hands on you and try to cast out of you that which is not even there."

"Do not ever hold against me, what others will do to you. It is because of who you are that you are possessed of My Holy Spirit. Amid rejection and heartache, I will be with you always, and bring you my pure joy. Which no man can ever take away."

I see with eyes so bright and clear,

The light of God's joy cast out my fear.

The devil's power has no part of me,

I am possessed of God and living free.

Satan cannot dwell within the same heart as the Lord,

He is defeated by the power of His two-edged sword.

For the Staff of his life will bind me in peace,

And the Rod of his Love will never cease.

So, try if you will, and say what you might;

But my twitch and my shout are not Satan's delight;

For the goodness of God is forever sewn;

In the fabric of His love and the grace He has shown.

What They Told Me

Over the years many have told me that because of my Tourette's that I cannot walk down certain avenues in my life:

From one person:

"Be content with the job you have. Not much future, but you'll never find a better position with your twitching."

From a lady at work:

"You'll never find true love with those tics of yours."

From parents at the playground, birthday parties and other events:

"Please, stay away from my kids."

From fellow Christians:

" If you were truly saved and truly a child of God, then you would pray and be healed. You must have no faith."

From fellow church members:

"Many are called, but few are chosen. You were not chosen."

"Can you sit outside, your noise is overwhelming, and we are recording our service"

What Jesus tells me:

"I love you so much, your twitch and shout will be my trumpet."

Exercises for my sense of humor

There can be a humorous side to Tourette's as well:

Late one evening, there was a knock at my door
"Could you please quiet your dog?"
"I don't have a dog, I have Tourette's"
~~
My window open to the back alley, Summer air an ease for my mind.
There was a knock on my back door. A sweet lady from across the alley asked
"Have you heard the cries of a wounded dog?"
"No" I said.
Everyday outside my window there was this lady looking for this dog.

In time, I found a better home closer to work.
While packing and moving my stuff,
The lady came out to talk to me.
"I'll miss you," she said.

I drew a breath and smiled.
"You know that dog you were looking for?
It was just me. I have Tourette's and was afraid
You would not understand."

"Oh!" She laughed.
"I'm glad I wasn't hearing things after all!"

. . .

The sweetest little girl

about 10 years old, came up

to my table in a restaurant.

She handed me some crackers,

"I think this will help your hiccups."

I thanked her and ate the crackers.

My head tics shook me back and forth.

The driver for my bus passed by,

thinking I was telling him

I did not want the bus.

~~

I have this twitch in my eyes, a blinking, sometimes winking tic.

One day while in a bar, trying to meet new friends,

this guy got all up in my face. He said, "Are you winking at me?!

What is your problem?" "No, I have Tourette's." He finally

understood, but not before I saw my life pass before me.

After church on Sunday:

"Why were you winking at me during the sermon?" asked the pastor.

~~

One place I felt safe and secure: as an actor performing on stage.

A person who knew me quite well remarked:

"I have never seen your Tourette's show up during a performance."

He was right.

Thorns

I said to Jesus, "Why can I not be, the man I long to be, instead of trying to be who I am not." And Jesus softly said to me "My dearest one, deny yourself take up your cross and follow me." Mathew 16:24

It was said to me, that Tourette's is not fatal, just uncomfortable; and the only reason to take any medication, is to make the world around me, more comfortable. I never took those dangerous medications, and the world around became distressing, and I moved into the shadows, alone.

Living with Tourette's is not easy, sometimes my tics have become so violent, that I have sprained my neck, and lost all feeling on my right side, caused severe headaches from the constant twitching of my head.

And at those times I felt that I wonder if I can make it, wonder if I can see it through the end of the day. And I became sad.

I lift my sadness to the Lord,

He brings a peaceful solace.

Touching the heart,

Encouraging the soul;

Elevating the spirit.

I draw my eyes up to the Lord,

The beauty that is His breath;

Bringing inspiration.

Finding Truth,

Knocking on freedom's door.

If we walk in the light, we can stand unashamed in his presence. We can completely expose our sins and know that God will accept us, into his Beloved.

-Wisdom Words

My Confidence

The one thing I often endured with Tourette Syndrome, was having an inability to find confidence in myself as a man. The things I could not do, became greater in my mind than the things I could do. But as I walked the pathway the Lord set for me, He built within me courage, some daring, and a whole lot of determination.

When times of trials come each day,

And I am lonely, down and far away,

When thoughts of peace have lost their way,

And sin sets in and causes me to stray,

I am going to keep on going and keep moving on,

Keep on working and praying until the battle is won.

For Satan's power has no part of me,

I am going to keep on running until I am living free.

So many changes within my soul,

"Lord, help me find what's real and make me whole.

Help me to see the truth and not pretend,

Bring me the confidence to see this to the end."

I am going to keep on going and keep moving on,

Keep on working and praying until the battle is won.

For Satan's power has no part of me,

I am going to keep on running until I am living free.

My love

I recall your beautiful smile when we first met,
The fun we had together. Ah these things I will not forget:
The light in your eyes and the little muskrat grin,
The joy that stopped my heart and made my spirit spin.

The quiet walks along Seaside's beach,
Nothing for us seemed out of reach,
The games we played, the poems we shared;
When life became sad you showed me you cared.

Entwined in our love and with much delight,
You gave a gift that brought joy to my sight.
I wrapped her in a swaddle, cradled her in my arms;
Ever since captured by my sweet daughter's charms.

As the years went by, attitudes began to change,
And the good times we had now became estranged;
The light in our life seemed to dim and fade,
And the fear that we felt is now unafraid.

I remember the hour that you walked away,
The sadness I felt overwhelmed me that day.
I tried so hard to understand it all,
What came to this place that led to the fall?

Ah my sweet dear I want you to know.
My love for you still, is always aglow.

The Rocking Chair

There have been so many times of deep anxiety and stress with Tourette's, that I have lived through many sleepless nights, and during those moments I often close my eyes and imagine The Lord rocking me to sleep.

Rock me my Lord in your rocking chair,
Hold me tight cast down my despair;
Dry my eyes from the stain of my tears,
Wash me in joy, cleanse all my fears.

There are troubles Lord, persecutions abound.
Falsely accused, my heart trampled to the ground;
The flesh is now bleeding, the spirit so broken;
But, through these trials, The Father has spoken:

"Come let me hold you, with all comfort and care,
Let me rock you, my child, in My rocking chair.

Show me your power by your strength, and I will show you my power, through my tears.

"And Jesus Wept." (John 11:35)

The Bondage Breaker, A Letter

Many times, I thought, how great it would be if I could go back in time and speak with those who impacted my life in negative ways and let them know that through it all I have been able to find a way to forgive them. But the years have gone by and most of the people are aged and worn with time, many are deceased. Through this letter to the church, I can at least put to rest, the years of turmoil my experiences caused me over the many years of my life.

There was a time, when I was very young in the Lord, back in the day when there was no name for something, we now call Tourette's Syndrome. It was during this time that God's word became true and faithful, "My son, never hold against me, what my people will do to you, stay strong and vigilant for mercy shall triumph over judgment."

So, it was that before long those who came to me and expressed their love and rejoiced that I was saved, became annoyed and said I was a distraction. They saw my tics, and sometimes heard my vocal sounds, and judged me.

One day I decided that maybe The Lord would remove these things from me if I went forward and sought prayer from the elders of the church. After all, I thought, does not the word of God say, "Confess your faults one to another and pray for one another that you might be healed?" And again, "If any be sick among you let him go to the elders of the church, that they may pray for you that you might be healed?" [James 5:14–16]

I went forward and stood before the church. The pastor looked at me and said, "You came to be prayed for and to be healed, however, know this, that you are possessed of Satan, and he needs to be cast from you."

So, they took me aside to a small out of the way room, and the elders surrounded me and began to command with a loud shout, for Satan to come out of me. It went on and on, for an hour or so, then suddenly silence. The tics were still there, the vocal sounds were even stronger, and I felt ashamed.

For days on end, they tried to cast the demons from me, then finally they said to me, "You won't let go, you are holding on, and we cannot have this in our church." So, they cast me out. But I remembered the words the Lord spoke to me, and I never held this against him. Jesus and I became close friends.

This, however, was not some isolated incident. Over the years, many who called themselves Christians told me I was not saved because "many are called but few are chosen." I went to find fellowship and inspiration from a Christian Commune, then called Shiloh, to New Covenant Fellowship, and a dozen others. They all started out with the same positive spin and ended with me being cast out into the wilderness, to fend for myself.
But Jesus was there for me, and he did bring a few good people into my life to see me through my darkest days.

To the Christian church I write:
Do not judge that which you do not know or understand, walk in love to those of us you call the "unlovelies."
Does not the word of God expressly say: "If we cannot love our brothers and sisters who we do see, how can we possibly love God who we cannot see." (1 John 4:20)
For when I needed you the most, you judged me greatly; when I came forward to be healed you cast me aside.
When I came to you for peace, you showed me tribulation. When I came to you to find hope, you gave me sadness. When I came to you for love, you defrauded me and gave me sorrow. And when I came to you for mercy, you showed me judgment.

Remember now the words of St Francis:

"Lord, make me an instrument of your peace,

Where there is hatred, let me sow love;

Where there is injury, pardon;

Where there is doubt, faith;

Where there is despair, hope;

Where there is darkness, light;

Where there is sadness, joy;

O Divine Master,

Grant that I may not so much seek

To be consoled as to console;

To be understood as to understand;

To be loved as to love.

For it is in giving that we receive;

It is in pardoning that we are pardoned;

And it is in dying that we are born to eternal life."

Dearest church let this be your tribute to the Lord and his kingdom:

Be what God has called you to be! Be a merciful church, full of joy and love for the unlovely people of the earth. They need salvation along with a little love and kindness.. For in the end mercy will triumph over judgment, but that same judgment will find its way to the unmerciful.

Lord, Grant me the strength to walk in love, without judgment, showing mercy on those less fortunate than myself. Help me to not walk in selfishness, and to give whatever I need to give, whatever I am able to give, whatever I am bound to give through your word of life. Let me show grace to those who have and still offend me, and allow me to give myself that same grace, when I offend others.

Finally, allow me to walk in forgiveness, to those who are in my past, who are no longer present in my future. To the church who caused me pain and hurt me so much.

If they are somewhere in this life, I pray that you forgive them. And that you have finally taught them how to show mercy to those who are the unlovely of this earth.

Bring blessings to their lives, joy to their souls, and forgive them who never thought to seek forgiveness.

May we remember always that mercy triumphs over judgment.
Be Blessed in the Lord. Amen

Part the Second

LIVING WITH TOURETTE'S
MY PATH TO GOD

Life has some many twists and turns, rejections and sorrow, we understand the choices we make impact who we are, and what we become. Look to your heart, let love abound within you, cherish your moment, and learn to forgive.
-Wisdom Words

The path to God is not without its hardship, rage and sometimes unflappable humor. Circumstances happen, sometimes difficult, other times downright hilarious, these are the times I believe that God is trying to teach me how to take life in stride.

Never be angry and outraged by those things in life that may trip you up and cause you to fall. For they are totally out of your control.

Therefore, I have learned many wonderful and powerful lessons, living with Tourette Syndrome. I learned how to love, how to respect others and accept them with all their faults and frailties. Not to judge without grace, or to assess without mercy. To treat others better than how I was rewarded.

Grace and Mercy this is where my path to God begins, and I hope for heaven's sake, it will never find an end.

Everything I have, everything I am, everywhere I belong, it is because of our Creator, our Lord. For the Greatness of God is found in the creation, the boundless seas, the highest mountains, for the greatness of God comes from His gentle breath which blew into us the spirit of life, and at that moment we became living souls. (Genesis 2:7)
—Quiet Observations

The Dwelling Place

On my Path to God I found trials and tribulation, but I met
an understanding God.

I have lived through time and space;
I have experienced the creation of the world,

And breathed into man the breath of life.
I have felt the strain of poverty,

The agony of war,
The sorrow of human frailty;

The destruction of peace,
The hideous existence of racism,

The sadness of hearing the voices of a million dying unborn children, crying out to be heard, then silenced.

I have felt the deep sacrifice of losing a son, who was mocked and scorned, and sent to a seemingly unjustified death.

Yet, I have also felt the joy, of seeing death destroyed, and the advent of eternal life. The warm embrace of peace, a glorious resurrection from the grave, the ascension of hope, the cross of wisdom.

"My children, I love you so much, that I died that you might find life, and when the trials of this life are over, I have made for you a dwelling place, where there is no more sorrow, no more pain, no tears casting off all fear. Won't you enter my joy?"

Habakkuk 3:17

On my path to God I discovered sorrow and sadness, but I learned to rejoice.

Although the fig tree shall not blossom,
Nor fruit be on the vine;
Though my labors will all fail,
And the field shall yield no wine.

Yet I will Rejoice in the Lord,
Indeed, I will rejoice in the Lord;
With uplifted voice unto Him I shall Rejoice.
Rejoicing in the God of my salvation.

Although the storms of life are raging on,
And I am tossed upon the sea,
Although the mountain seems too high to climb,
And its cold sharp wind is blinding me.

Let us Rejoice in the Lord,
Indeed, I will rejoice in the Lord;
With uplifted voice unto Him I shall Rejoice.
Rejoicing in the God of my salvation.

Unafraid

On my path to God I found I was lonely and afraid, yet I overcame it.

Alone, I was afraid to see myself as someone God has made,

To find my wealth, not in the riches of this world,

Nor in the wisdom of man,

But in this new birth; to be as the world began.

There beneath the summers tree,

I lay hidden within its deepest shade;

Within myself to be, as one that is unafraid.

As a man, for me living with Tourette's sometimes I think to myself, I have never accomplished what I set out to do in life; I look to other people and become jealous at what they have done and think I have done nothing worthwhile.

But then I look at all that God has given me, a lovely child, good friends, and a solid foundation we call Christ. Then I realize that I am a man who is truly blessed.
—Quiet Observations

Double Mindedness

On my path to God there were times I wanted to quit and just walk away; but I persevered.

There comes a time and place, when each man decides in his mind;
To enter God's grace, or to leave it all behind.

The man who enters in, shall find peace through his days;
But the double-minded man, will grow unstable in all his ways.

Now, throughout my life, I found emptiness and strife;
I just could not understand why I was not free.

In my mind, I wondered why, in my heart I began to cry,
as I heard the voice of God say to me:

"Turn and be converted, and I will heal you;
Open your eyes and seek the truth.
I will bless you abundantly, you will see and be made free.
Turn, be converted and be made whole."

We are always and should be in constant change, we will never be perfect, but we can strive for it constantly.
-Wisdom Words

To the Fallen

Sometimes the path of God is filled with many trials and tribulations, and when we fall, and fall we will; turning against the one who gives us life. Let us seek to revive our courage, advancing forward, unencumbered.

My Child why have you turned against me, crucified me once again
and put me to an open shame.

Do you not remember, my suffering? Do not forget that with every
crack of the whip upon my back; I cried for you.

Every thorn pressed down upon my head, blood falling into my eyes,
from that crown of thorns, I bled for you.

Each step I took laden with the Cross of hope; consuming all your burdens,
The fears, shame and despair. I was in heaviness for you.

And with each strike of the nail in my hands and feet,
I suffered that you might find peace;

Remember always dear fallen one; that in the beginning my Father,
blew into your nostrils the breath of His life, and you became a living soul.

Do you not know that with my last breath, I breathed into you a new life?
Born again, that you might live with me forever.

The Bay

On this path to God, can you imagine for a moment, what it would be like to play on the sands of paradise? One in which His promise of all things becoming new, "for the earth is the Lords and the fullness, thereof; the world, and they that dwell therein." (Psalms 24:1)
I Close my eyes, and see, the sweetness of paradise, a place I can call home.

In the Bay the sky is bright and clear,

The oceans waves are soft and settled,

Sand crabs and jelly fish washed upon the beach;

Oysters on the pearled shore.

Seagull's, strutting;

Squawking, strutting some more.

Then fly away.

People passing each other, tip their hats, smile and say hello,

For there are no strangers here.

Children Running,

Laughing;

Drawing in the sand:

A funny face, a heart with an arrow, a sand castle strong and mighty,

Footprints of folly.

Righteous and holy, God from His Front Porch, watching it all.

Trust

The path to God leads to trusting the Lord, finding our Salvation.

Praise the Lord – Trust in him
He knows your every thought,
your ideas,
your innermost being.

Praise the Lord and trust in Him,
For your food,
Shelter,
The job you seek,
For fellowship.

Praise the Lord and trust in Him,
With all your faith,
And if you have little, then trust in Him for more.
For this faith is our foundation,
The positive proof that God is who he says he is.

Believe;
And you will find Salvation in a world, you never even knew existed.

It is because of Human Frailty, that causes us, to wrongly judge that which we do not understand.

Moments of forgotten days, Memories of sorrow and tears. In a search for love, beyond those ageless fears. The past is gone; A touch of life still lingers on. As before my waking eyes, my God appears.
-Wisdom Words

Part the Third

LIVING WITH TOURETTE'S
FINDING LOVE, ACCEPTANCE,
AND FORGIVENESS

Throughout my life, living with Tourette's, for me has been filled with enormous hurt, trauma, and sadness. And yet The Lord has called me to walk in forgiveness, toward those who brought this sorrow to my life. This has been the most difficult for me, but at the same time as I have learned to forgive, I also have received blessings and friendships beyond what I thought was possible. Forgiveness is the biggest bondage breaker there is, embrace it, and win your freedom.

Life has some many twists and turns, rejections and sorrow, we understand the choices we make impact who we are, and what we become. Look to your heart, let love abound within you, cherish your moment, and learn to forgive.

Give thanks for what you have, be happy with who you are, and when you stand before the Father, he will say "My good and faithful servant, enter into the joy of the lord, for the gates of heaven are open to you."

For without forgiveness, there can be no love. It is not your human love, that makes your life complete, but forgiveness that completes your love.
— A Simple Truth

Forgiveness

Throughout my years,
And the many tears;
The sorrow and the pain,
And all the hurt that follows me
Down this memory lane.

Of all things, I have battled through,
With the sinners to the saints,
From casting out the evil one,
And focusing on their complaints.

The one thing that remains so honestly true
That helps me to make it emphatically through;
That the goodness in life, that I know I can live,
As I have made it my purpose to simply forgive.

What God Wants

The worst thing I can do,
Is to do what others have done to me;

Therefore:
I choose to forgive
I choose Mercy over intolerance;
I choose grace over ignorance.

Forgiveness, mercy and grace,
Is what the Lord has shown to me, abundantly.
So, I will share His generosity with others,
Let God's mercy be upon you and give you grace.

Here, let me show you mercy,
Let me give you grace,
And shine the light of He
That will put a smile upon your face.

Miracle of Heart

*True healing is not in finding it from Tourette's itself, but in that of the heart.
I can live with this disability, if my soul and spirit find comfort in redemption.*

There are hurts that lie within every woman and every man;
There is a question that begins "I wonder if I can."
For Jesus supplies our every need, He is our all in all,
When he comes to comfort me, all these hurts begin to fall.

The Tongue can no man tame it is unruly and unwise;
It kills an army swiftly and creates a thousand lies.
But, if Jesus can change a raging storm, or calm and angry sea,
He can change the hearts of men and turn it to victory.

The answer to the question that all men truly seek,
Lay hidden in the hurting hearts of the helpless and the weak;
Who God raised up from a lonely grave, for all the world to see;
The gift of love that Jesus gave, is the gift that sets us free.

He will cleanse our mind, and take away all sorrow,
Ease every pain, and bring a bright tomorrow;
Right there in our despair we know, He will not depart;
For the healing of ourselves is a miracle of heart.

The Peacemaker

Tourette's brings me turmoil and strife, but I am learning to find peace.

You can write a song of peace,
Give it words that will not cease;
Let its sound keep moving on,
Sing out and sing it strong.

Follow peace down quiet streams,
Living waters of our dreams;
Follow peace throughout this land,
Call it out and take a stand.

Shout it out just one more time,
Sing out peace and let it rhyme;
Let truth prevail and you will sow
The seeds of peace that will surely grow.

The Rose of Sharon

Finding love has been difficult for me almost impossible. Because my tics and noises get in the way of relationships. The love that the Lord has given me is enough to sustain me.

Behold the glory of the flower,

Whose blossoms are filled with life.

Each day hour by hour,

Bringing joy where there is strife.

Behold the flower that is free.

He grows but never strains.

There standing alone in dignity

Drinking the heavens rain.

Lovely is His tender smile,

Within a heart filled with grace;

Such peace no man can ever defile,

For His eyes shine light upon his face.

Now we behold the Glory of this Flower,

He is the Rose of Sharon, the Glory of God's power.

A Beautiful Love

Love, as it grows from a tiny seed,

And blossoms into a quiet beauty;

A spectrum of color living carefree.

To feel the warmth deep within its bosom.

As it grows no more,

Knowing the fullness of its life

Will it wither and die?

It shall rise above the dust,

To become the beauty from ashes.

Sounds of Laughter

*To find joy and gladness amid turmoil, when my tics are bad, I have learned
to laugh in the joy of the Lord.*

Sounds of Laughter in my mind,
Tells of joy that I find.
It echoes through this childish brain;
Sounds of laughter falls like rain.

And now my spirit moving free;
God's pure Joy brings life to me.
To know that sorrow now has passed,
I found my joy now, at last.

Raised up hands in surrender, I sigh
Like a strong and proud eagle, I soar, and I fly.
Now I behold His sweet laughing face,
His laughter of joy falls as grace.

Give thanks for what you have, be happy with who you are, and when you stand before the Father, he will say "My good and faithful servant, enter into the joy of the lord, for the gates of heaven are open to you."
-Wisdom Words.

As the Trumpet Sounds

Sometimes with my Tourette's I pretend to be God's Trumpet

Green leaves of summer Fade into fall;
Hear the Shout of the angels and the trumpet call.

As earths tattered weeds plant its seeds beneath the fertile sod;
This sinful earth got her birth from a sinless God.

As the Trumpet Sounds, Every Man, and woman, girl and boy,
shall bow before our King of joy.

Earth shall pass, our name shall be changed,
the things of the past shall be re-arranged.

Old lives will fade beneath earths sullen sod.
Reaching out to touch the mighty face of God.

My Integrity

I noticed when I finished my shopping and looked over the sales receipt, that the clerk forgot to charge me for one small item. So, I went back to the store, to pay for it.

I said to the him, "Sir, you forgot to charge me for this item, so I would like to pay for it now."

The clerk replied, "You did not have to bring it back to me, nobody would have bothered to even notice the difference.

I replied to the clerk: "Sir, my integrity is not for sale." With that I paid for the item and went about my day.

Be Strong and teachable, Honesty and integrity will become your closest friends.

Without honesty, trust cannot prevail, Without trust. integrity will all but fail.

I can be the wealthiest, the most famous, and even the most beautiful, Without Integrity "I am nothing!"

Amid the noise of war, the violence and rage, the sorrow and the sadness. The one thing common to all of us, is the need for a friend.
-Wisdom Words

Always My Friend

You will always be a Father to me, God.
You will always be a Father to me;
Though this world will put you down,
Though they stripped you of Your Crown,
You will always be my Father to me.

You will always be my Savior to me, God
You will always be my Savior to me;
Though they nailed you to the tree,
I am walking in victory;
You will always be my Savior to me.

You will always be a friend to me, God;
You will always be a friend to me;
Though this world will shut you out,
To me there is no doubt
You will always be a friend, To me.

Lyrical

I See the sunshine over the hillside,

mellowed in a silence of spring;

Right there I see Jesus walking over the mountain,

With a rose in His hand for me.

Blue Rose of heaven, treasure purer than gold, Laden with love, ne'er growing old,

As the moonlight greets morning over the hill,

Jesus is walking there, still.

The Earth is the Lords. . ..

Behold the wind, that mighty wind which blows and moves
Like a tempest toward the shore, to split the leaves of the trees,
Clapping their hands with joyous delight.
This wind is alive a thundering voice of praise.

Exhorting the air to breathe praises to our God.
Hear the wind, God's spiritual voice,
The glory of glories, that with one deep sound,
Reeling to and fro, bringing turmoil upon the earth
And troubling the mighty sea.

Sing gentle wind Unto God's great mountain.
Gaze through its mind at all its high rich fountains.
Walk through the garden richly adorned.
With fresh fruit and figs, the wheat and the corn.

Touch the sweet bird that soars in her flight,
Bow to the Word, in the world a great light.
For in His goodness he has given to thee,
His grace in all sweetness, a life living free.

Behold now the sea,
rolling waves, white foam, Blue waters,
Moving, ever moving emotion, over sands;
Pounding the once mighty rocks into particles of stone and pebble.

Hear the voice of the sea, roaring her praises to the Lord:
I am the sea, created by the hands of the living God'!

I parted for Moses to let his people go
crushing the might men of pharaohs army.

I was the scene of many a baptism,
when the Lord went down in me, I sang in Joyous delight.

I lifted Him up and let him walk upon me,
I saw rise above the clouds His eternal love and majesty.

Beholding the glory in His eyes
Which the world cries, Maranatha, our Lord comes.

And when He comes, therefore I the sea will be no more,
But until such time, my savor is my salt, my temper rage.

Behold the creatures of the earth,
For the eagle and the ant, the lion and the lamb,
Generation to generations of living ever-loving beings;
Rejoicing and becoming glad, for theirs is the earth and all its glory.
—Amen

As birds of the air we can see a thousand horizons, as time an end to all our Labor.

—Just a thought

My Tomorrow

I travel to the ocean with my bags and empty sorrow,
To rest upon the sands of time and dream of my tomorrow.

For Jesus is a friend to me that comes so close to comfort me
To touch His gentle hands upon my mind.

As I sit and ponder through tunnels of the ages
Thinking of this passage I write on empty pages.

For Jesus is a friend to me that comes so close to comfort me
To touch His gentle hands upon my mind.

Now I leave this place in his true grace now touched by brilliant light;
Its sword of truth, which brightly slays the darkness of the night.

For Jesus is a friend to me that comes so close to comfort me
To touch His gentle hand upon my mind.

The Blind Man and The Stranger

The blind man sat by the side of the road and their he felt the warmth of the sun upon his face; and he did hear the wind and the roaring of the sea; smelling the fragrance of the trees and flowers; with his senses, he can touch the landscape, and behold the beauty of the Creation.

Slowly his frail body, laid down in the tufts of the grass, and with his hands he felt its softness, and between his fingers the wetness of the drops of dew, each finger being lovingly cleansed by the sweetness of nature's oil.

Now laying in the still silence of the morning, he listened to the quiet. And this quiet spoke to him, in soft refrains, and gently whispered things that only he could understand.

The blind man was touched by the quiet, and he smiled, and laughed, because he knew that in time, he will see, the blue of the sea, the green of the grass and the yellow of the sun. But little did he know, that time was sooner than he could ever imagine.

And so, it was on that bright spring day, laying down taking in the warmth that surrounded him. Suddenly, without warning, he felt a small, slight, tremor from the earth, beneath his tired frame, the earth began to shake. Not a violent quake, just a gentle wave, like a little child being tenderly rocked in a cradle.

Then the quiet was pierced, with sounds of music; the shaking of the tambourine. The sound kept getting closer, closer. louder and louder, the sounds of jubilation reaching its crescendo, voices of many singing out in the morning; then suddenly, fading into silence. Quiet, Still.

As the blind man rose to his feet, he knew he was surrounded by what seemed to be an army. Who were they? What did they want from him? He wondered. Curiously he felt no danger, just a quiet peace.

Then in the silence, he heard footsteps, walking toward him. Then come to a stop, he felt upon his face the breath of a stranger. Who was this man he was now facing? "Who are you stranger?" The blindman asked. And the stranger said, "I am He who made the lame to walk and raised Lazarus from the dead. Changed water to wine."

The blind man answered, "I have heard of these miracles, and often dreamed of one day being able to see again."

And the stranger said, "Do you have the faith to believe, for my people hear my voice, do you know who I am."

The blind man replied, "I believe that you are no stranger." And with tears in his eyes he explained, "I know now and believe, that you are Jesus of Nazareth, the Son of the Living God, who I only knew about through stories and legends told. And with that the blind man, fell to his knees.

He felt a gentle hand reach out and lift him to his feet. And Jesus covered his eyes, and with an ever so soft touch, "Your faith has made you whole, for even though you could not see yet you believed."

And so, it was on this bright spring day, the life of this one insignificant man, who dreamed of seeing the simplicity of creation, looked up and saw the blue of the sky, the high mountains. Thus, lowering his eyes, the green of the grass, and the blue waves of the sea, its white foam, and the gentle wind brushing ever so slightly, through the trees.

But what he will remember most about this day, is that, as he opened his eyes, the first thing he saw, what he did see, was the Glory of Jesus the Face of the free.

Epilogue

CONCLUSION OF THE WHOLE MATTER

I have learned, that living with Tourette's or any kind of disability, does not have to be horrible, it sometimes can be very fulfilling; gaining from it, wisdom, long suffering, patience, mercy, and sometimes unconditional love.

Just a Joyful Noise

How Beautiful God's morning Touching the spirit with light,

The light the glory of the day.

A prelude found in delight.

A simple peace,

A quiet love;

A melody in a song that is life;

In an overture to Joy.

To God Be the Glory

To God be the Glory and all Glory to His Son,
Where He goes
I will follow, after;
Where he walks, I will run.

I will be not a stranger,
In this land called eternity.
To God be the Glory,
And the victory.

Being Me

It took me a long time to realize, that having Tourette's is not a prison sentence, being locked up and trying to hide, from an unforgiving world, often feeling worthless. I decided that for the sake of inner peace, to just be myself and realize, that I am not such a bad guy after all.

Some men hope to be
The greatest of mankind'.

Others reach for fame
And sadness is what they find.

Some reach up at crowded skies
And try and touch their star;

Still others try so very hard,
To be greater than who they are.

But all I know, is who I am,
And what I hope to be.

For all it's worth I think,
I would rather be just me.

Twitch and Shout, Hallelujah, Amen

I say to myself what is this thing all about
I look to my soul and I twitch, and I shout.

Then there's the saint who has shut me out
Then I look to his heart and I twitch, and I shout.

I looked at my friend who walked sadly away,
"Though I twitch, and I shout won't you please stay."

"I cannot stay and be your friend,"
For Your twitch and shout will never end.

I fell to my knees and I prayed, and I wept,
And I Twitched, and I shouted, even as I slept.

I looked to the Lord for the now and the then,
"when is the time for the how and the when?"

"In my haven, my child, you will find the now, has been,
Your Twitch and your Shout will be your Hallelujah, Amen"

In thinking over the many years of my life,

I find myself having no regrets;

Through all my pain, hurts, rejection, trials, tribulations, and even my Tourette's, If I have the choice to do it over again, I would not change a thing.

For in all of this, it has made me the person I am today,

And the man who God wants me to be.

And when I leave this earth, and meet my Savior face to face;

Know this, that upon my tombstone will read:

"He Truly was a man of Grace"

Now this is the conclusion of the whole matter:

In our struggle for freedom, and our fight against evil, if we live by the sword, we die by the sword, but what happens if we live by the cross?

Take up your cross and follow Jesus.

Find your way to the Lord, once there, hang on to His coattails and enjoy the ride.

Hallelujah, Amen!!

www.ingramcontent.com/pod-product-compliance
Lightning Source LLC
LaVergne TN
LVHW051707080426
835511LV00017B/2769